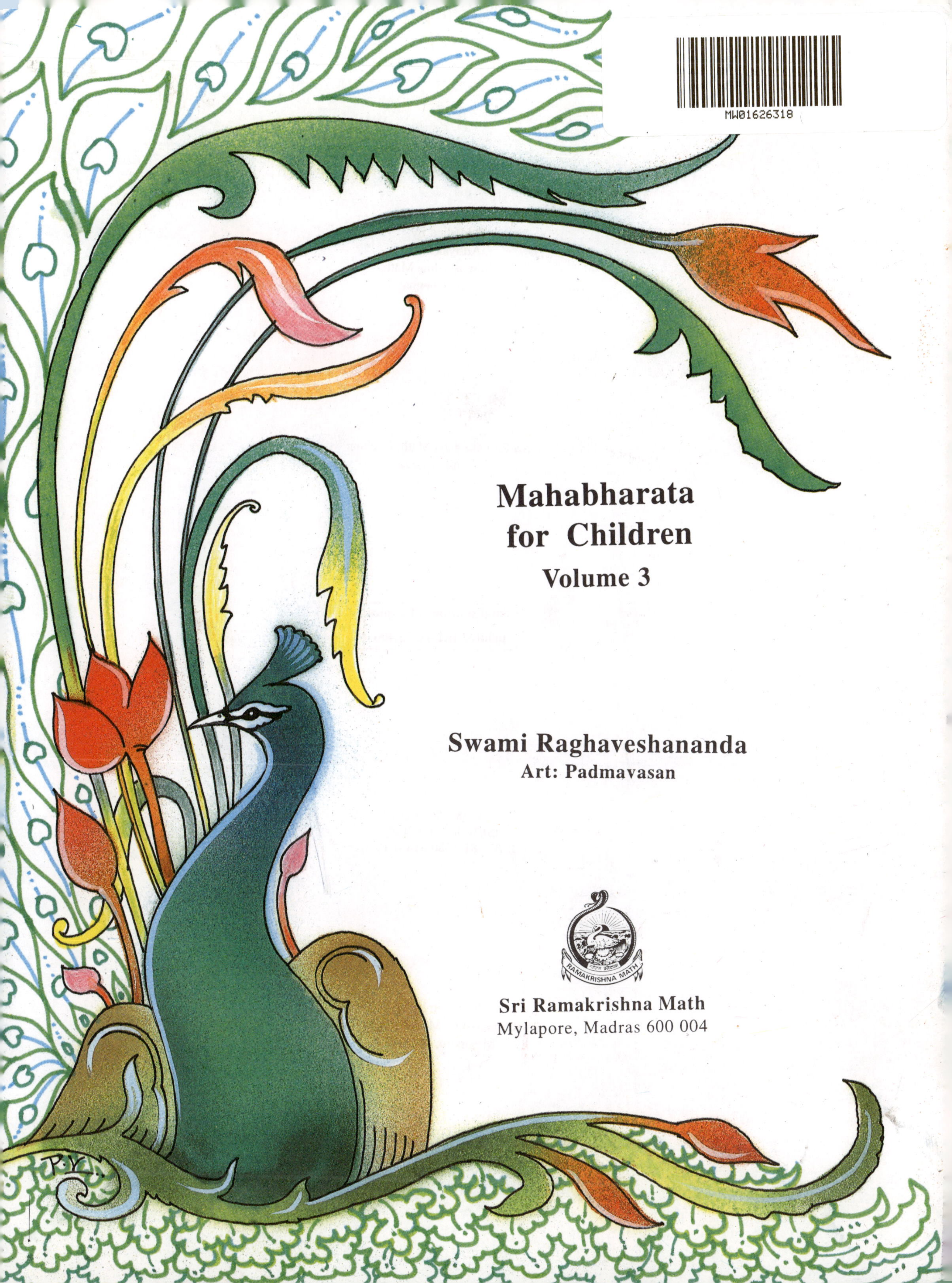

Mahabharata for Children

Volume 3

Swami Raghaveshananda

Art: Padmavasan

Sri Ramakrishna Math

Mylapore, Madras 600 004

Published by
Adhyaksha
Sri Ramakrishna Math
Mylapore, Chennai-4

Total number of copies printed before 73,400

XV-3M 3C-9-2011
ISBN 81-7120-445-7
ISBN 81-7120-314-0 (Set)

Printed in India at
Sri Ramakrishna Math Printing Press
Mylapore, Chennai-4

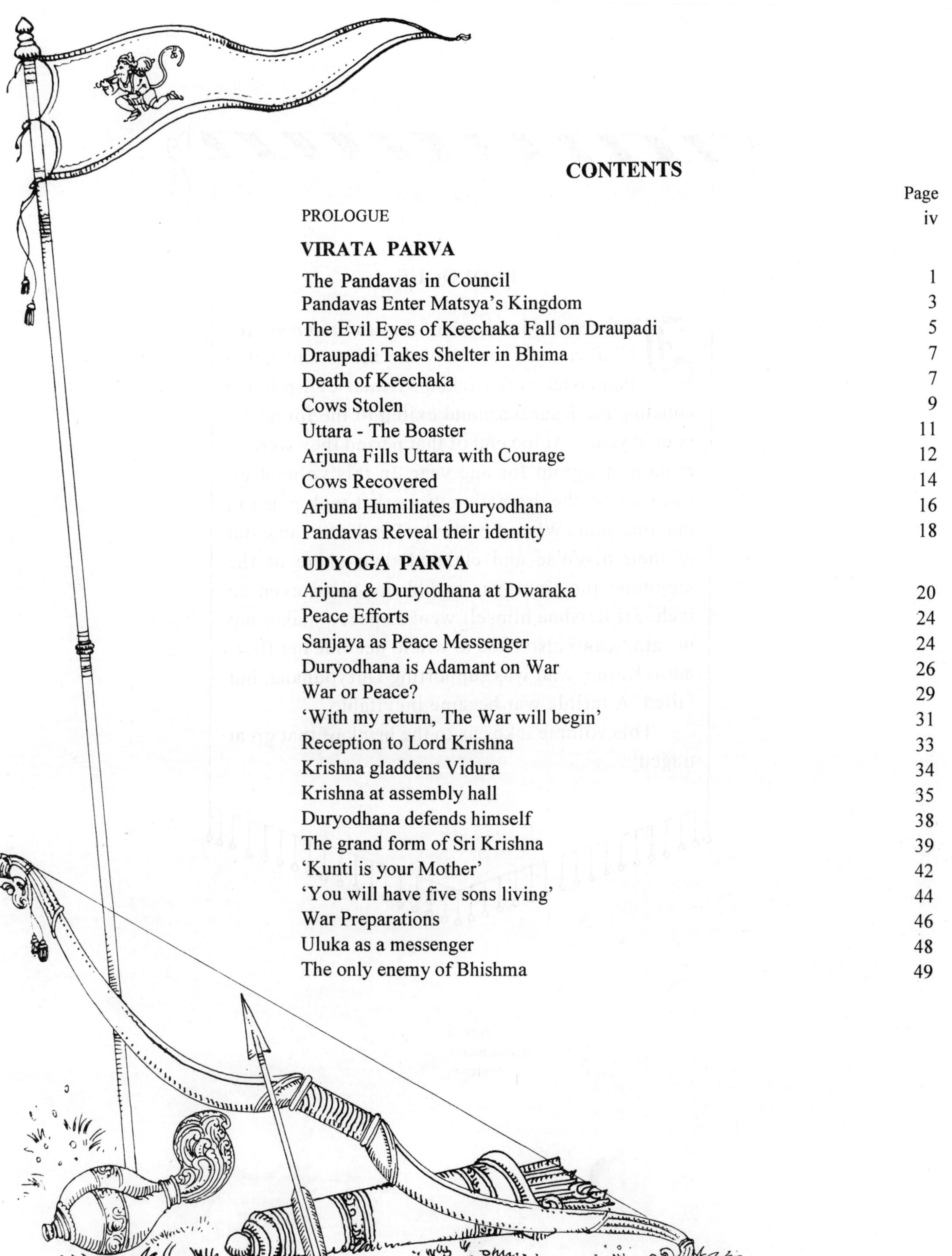

CONTENTS

PROLOGUE

In the second volume of the *Mahabharata for Children* we saw how the brave and noble Pandavas were tricked by their evil-minded cousins, the Kauravas, and exiled to the forest for twelve years. At the end of that period they were to remain incognito for one year. In this volume we can witness the dramatic events that took place in that one year. When finally the Pandavas came out of their disguise and claimed their share of the kingdom, the Kauravas would not yield even an inch. Sri Krishna himself went as peace-maker but in vain. Kunti also tried to win to her side her first-born, Karna, who was supporting Duryodhana, but failed. A teribile war became inevitable.

This volume takes us to the brink of that great tragedy.

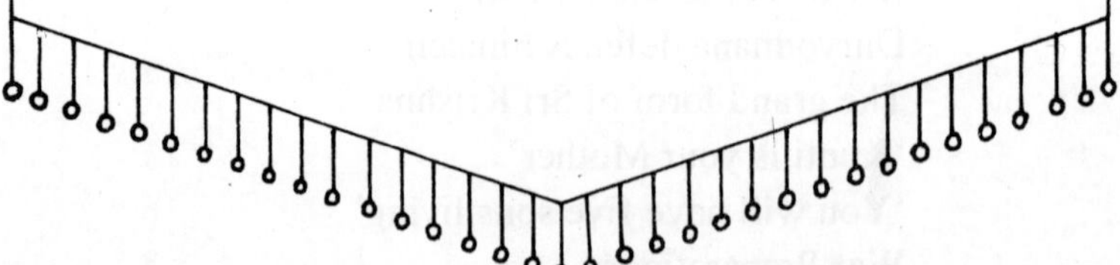

VIRATA PARVA

THE PANDAVAS IN COUNCIL

The Pandavas, along with Draupadi and Dhaumya, sat in a lonely place and began to consider their future plans. Yudhishthira said, "Think of a place, Arjuna, where we may stay for a year without being recognised by our enemies."

Arjuna said, "I can suggest any number of charming, remote spots which surround the kingdom of the Kurus: Panchala, Chedi, Matsya, Surasena, Malla, Saurashtra, Avanti and Kuntirashtra. Any of these will do."

Yudhishthira said, "The aged Virata, the king of Matsya is powerful, charitable and righteous. His country appeals to me. I shall disguise myself as a brahmin and call myself Kanka, the gambler. I shall make them happy with games of dice. If the king asks for my credentials, I shall say, 'I was a friend of Yudhishthira, dear as his life to him. O Bhima, what is your plan?" Bhima said, "I shall present myself as a cook named Vallala. I am an expert cook. I shall please Virata by preparing dainty dishes such as he has never tasted before."

Yudhishthira turned towards Arjuna and praising him for his exploits asked him, "What profession do you propose to take up? How can you hide your valour?"

Arjuna replied, "I prefer to be a eunuch. To hide the bow string marks on my arms

is indeed difficult, but I shall try to cover them with bangles. I shall wear bangles made of white conchshell. I shall braid my hair like a woman. I shall teach the women of the palace singing and dancing. I shall seek work saying that I used to serve Draupadi in Yudhishthira's court."

"What about you Nakula, so graceful and modest?" asked Yudhishthira.

"I shall work in King Virata's stables. Horses are ever dear to me even as they are to you. I shall name myself Damagranthi."

"And you, Sahadeva?"

"The keeper of his cows, Tantripal," said Sahadeva.

Yudhishthira ultimately turned towards Draupadi and said, "O Draupadi, you are dearer to us all than our life. You should be cherished like a mother and respected like an elder sister. How will you appear? You are a princess wholly unaccustomed to hard work. You are nobly born and tenderly nurtured."

Draupadi looking at him smilingly said, "I shall be Sairandhri in the court of the queen of Virata — a companion and attendant of the princess. I shall tell them that I served as a maid-in-waiting in Yudhishthira's palace."

Yudhishthira said, "Very well, but you know very little of the ways of the world. Be careful. Behave in such a way that the wicked and sinful men have no chance of casting lustful looks at you."

Yudhishthira then turned towards Dhaumya and other Brahmins and said, "It will be proper for you all to spend your time in the court of Drupada." Yudhishthira was now satisfied with these arrangements. Then they took leave of Dhaumya and other Brahmins. Buckling on their sheathed swords and wearing lizardskin and finger protectors, the Pandavas proceeded towards the river Yamuna's southern bank, the land of the Matsyas.

"I see tracks here," said Draupadi, "Virata's metropolis is seen in the distance. Let us rest here for the night. I am too tired to walk any further." Yudhishthira asked Arjuna to carry Draupadi on his shoulders, so that they could cover some more distance and reach the capital. Arjuna carried her and they all reached Virata's capital.

"Where shall we keep our weapons?" asked Yudhishthira. Arjuna said, "Near the cremation ground on that hill is a huge Sami tree. Let us hide our weapons among its tangled branches." Nakula climbed the tree and tied the weapons high up in the strong branches. They were tied up in such a way that it looked like a corpse from a distance. Some shepherds asked them what they were doing. The Pandavas said, "It is the corpse of our mother, who died at the age of one hundred and eighty years. It is our family custom to dangle corpses from trees." Then they entered the capital. Yudhishthira selected for himself and his brothers the code names of Jaya, Jayanta, Vijaya, Jayatsena and Jayatbala.

PANDAVAS ENTER MATSYA'S KINGDOM

Yudhishthira, while about to enter the city of Virata, mentally prayed to the Divine Mother Durga and sang hymns in praise of Her. The Divine Mother, pleased with his devotion, appeared before them and said, "O Yudhishthira, I give you my blessing. You will recover your lost kingdom very soon." Yudhishthira entered the court of Virata. King Virata seeing Yudhishthira entering the court like Indra, turned to his advisers and said, "Who is he, who appears like a king even though he is without slaves, chariots and elephants?"

Yudhishthira approached the king and humbly said, "I am a Brahmin, having lost everything, come to you for help."

"You are very welcome, but do tell me who you are and from where you have come here," said Virata. Yudhishthira replied, "I am a Brahmana, formerly a friend of Yudhishthira. My name is Kanka. I am good at the game of dice."

Virata assured him of a place in his palace. He at once accepted Yudhishthira as his personal adviser and gave him full freedom to lead a very honourable life. Virata's magnanimity was such that he said, "This kingdom is as much yours as it is mine."

Next entered Bhima. He walked in like a lion, holding in hand a cooking ladle and long spoon. Virata was astonished to see his beauty and valour. Bhima said, "Sir, I am a cook named Vallala. I am an expert in the culinary arts. Please appoint me as your cook."

The king said, "I do not believe that cooking is your business. You shine like Indra. You seem to be well-built with grace, beauty and strength."

Bhima said, "O King, Once I was a cook of Yudhishthira. I am not only an expert cook but also a good wrestler. I shall always entertain you by fighting with elephants and lions."

Virata said, "You shall be in charge of our kitchen."

Draupadi called herself as Sairandhri and took up the job of serving Sudhekshana, Virata's queen. She lived in the inner apartments of the palace as a maid and companion, engaging herself in all works. One day, King Virata, saw a person standing before him. Attracted by this, he sent for him and asked him who he was. The man said, "Once I was looking after the cows of the Pandavas. Given a chance, I shall gladly serve you." Thus Sahadeva secured a job as one in charge of the cows of the palace.

Next to appear at the gate was a tall and handsome person wearing feminine ornaments, large golden earrings and conchshell bangles, with long hair flowing down his neck. Approaching the king, he said, "My name is Brihannala. I can sing, dance and play musical instruments. Let me be the dance teacher to princess Uttara. Pray, do not ask me how I became a eunuch. It is a very painful story." "I shall not probe your past. You are appointed as you desire," said the king.

Then came Nakula introducing himself as an expert in the care of horses. As he too was winsome, he was immediately appointed. Thus lived the Pandavas in the kingdom of Matsya, counting the days. Ten months passed in this way.

THE EVIL EYES OF KEECHAKA FALL ON DRAUPADI

Draupadi who was used to luxury was now compelled to wait on others. She did her best in satisfying the Queen Sudekshana and the other ladies of the palace. During the last days of her stay, she happened to attract the attention of Keechaka, brother of Sudekshana and commander-in-chief of Virata's army. Burning with intense desire, he went to his sister and said, "Who is this new girl? Her beauty intoxicates me like fresh wine. That she renders this kind of service to you is quite unacceptable to me. Let me take her." Then from there, he went to Draupadi and said, "Who are you? Your beauty is beyond words. I will renounce all my wives and make them all your servants. I will be a slave to you and be ever obedient to you. Please accept me." Draupadi said in reply, "I am Sairandhri of a low caste. Besides, I am already married. It does not behove you to seek to marry me. This conduct does not seem proper for one in your position." But Keechaka was possessed by an irresistible passion. He said again, "Look at me. I have everything that people desire — youth, good looks and wealth. In heroism, I have no rival on earth. I shall confer on you my entire kingdom. Accept me and enjoy this kingdom with me." Draupadi said, "O wicked-minded Keechaka! Do not imagine I am helpless and alone. I am always protected by five Gandharvas. If they are provoked they will destroy you. It is not good for you to bring destruction on yourself." Rejected thus, Keechaka went to his sister and said, "Sister, I am in love with this girl. You must find a way for me to marry her." Taking pity on her brother, Sudekshana said, "At the time of the festival, I will order her to go to your room on the pretext of fetching food and wine for me. At that time, humour her and bring her around. Cajole her into accepting you." But when Sudekshana told her to bring food and drink from Keechaka's house Draupadi said, "I shall not go anywhere near him. How utterly shameless he is!" Sudeshana said, "Knowing that you have been sent by me, he will not harm you." Praying to the Sun God for protection, fearing and trembling, Draupadi went to Keechaka's house to fetch wine. The Sun God pleased with her prayer ordered a Rakshasa to protect her and from that time the Rakshasa always stood by the side of Draupadi, keeping himself invisible. Draupadi, praying, 'May my fidelity to my husbands protect me,' entered Keechaka's house like a frightened deer.

"O! you have come. I am fortunate tonight," said Keechaka, "I have bracelets, golden chains, beautiful gems and jewels for you. Accept them as my gift. I have also prepared a very fine bed for you. Sit with me and let us drink this sweet wine together". "I am sent by the queen to fetch wine," said Draupadi, "Give me the wine quickly." Keechaka said, "Others will take care of it." Saying thus, Keechaka seized her right hand. She said, "I have never been unfaithful to my husbands even in my heart." Nevertheless, Keechaka seized her by the end of her upper garment as she tried to run away. Furious with anger, she hurled him to the ground. Then Draupadi ran to Yudhishthira in the court, to seek his protection. But Keechaka pursued her, caught her by her hair, threw her on the ground and kicked her in Yudhishthira's presence.

At that moment, the invisible Rakshasa shoved aside Keechaka who fell down unconscious. Bhima was also, witnessing it. He was wild with rage. Gnashing his teeth he rushed forward to kill Keechaka. Yudhishthira, fearing that their identity might be discovered, pressed Bhima's thumb and commanded him to desist. Yudhishthira said,

"Go, cut down a tree for fuel and start cooking our food." Draupadi turned to King Virata and said, "He has insulted me, Sir, in your own court. I am the faithful wife of five Gandharvas. Is there no Dharma in this kingdom? Does no one protest?" Virata said, "I do not know even the cause of your quarrel. How can I judge who is guilty?" Then the courtiers, having heard everything, praised Draupadi repeatedly exclaiming, "Well done, well done". They reproached Keechaka bitterly for his disgraceful conduct. Yudhishthira with drops of perspiration trickling down his face said, " Go to the inner apartments. The wives of heroes endure pain for the sake of their husbands. Probably your Gandharva husbands do not consider this as a proper time to punish the wicked. They will surely assuage your sorrow and punish him who has wronged you."

DRAUPADI TAKES SHELTER IN BHIMA

Sairandhri ran to her apartments weeping. There she reflected for a while, "What shall I do? Where shall I go?" She thought of Bhima, muttering, 'No one else can properly revenge.' At night she went to Bhima who was snoring like a lion in sleep. She roused him from his bed and spoke to him softly and sweetly.

"You are sleeping like one dead when I am in such mortal peril. That wretch, Keechaka, has attempted to dishonour me. You should not leave him alive after this. I cannot bear this suffering any longer. You must kill that wretch Keechaka at once. For all our sakes, I do this menial job. I do not mind it. Now look at my palms which had earlier served Mother Kunti and all of you. By serving these people my palms are cracked and stained. And Keechaka is chasing me. I warned him that my five Gandharva husbands would kill him if he tried to molest me. But he is not at all bothered about it . He is a wicked man. He is arrogant and lustful. You must kill him. If you do not kill him, I will kill myself by consuming poison."

So saying Sairandhri covered her face with her hands and wept uncontrollably. It was too much for Bhima to bear. He took her hands and caressed her affectionately. He had mentally determined the next course of action and said, "Do not worry, Draupadi. I shall not bother about Yudhishthira's promise or Arjuna's advice. I pledge to kill Keechaka tomorrow. You meet him and invite him to come alone to the dancing hall." Draupadi felt greatly relieved.

DEATH OF KEECHAKA

Next morning, Keechaka met her and said, "Did you notice that none came to your rescue, when I kicked you in the open hall in the presence of everyone? I am the real ruler here and Virata is king only in name. It will be better for you to accept me and marry me. Then I shall be your servant and you can enjoy this entire kingdom." Sairandhri pretended to agree. she said, "I agree to your suggestion, but I am afraid of my husbands. Let us make a deal. No one must know our affairs, not even your friends and relatives. Promise this and I shall come." Keechaka agreed to the condition delightedly. Sairandhri invited him to meet her in the dancing hall that very night. That night Keechaka adorned himself with fine clothes, garlands and ornaments. He sprinkled rich

perfumes on his person and proceeded towards the dancing hall. Finding the doors open, he gently entered the place, his heart panting in joyous expectancy.

In the very dim light, he saw there someone lying on a cot and gently laid his hands on the person. Bhima who was waiting there for Keechaka jumped up from the cot and seized him by his hair. Keechaka, shocked and surprised, boldly grappled with Bhima. He was no coward; he was now fighting for his dear life. Bhima fell on the floor with a thud. He got up as quick as lightning and hit Keechaka hard on the chest. The fighting went on. At last Bhima caught the unfortunate Keechaka in his arms and pushed him to the ground and slowly strangled him. Keechaka could not escape from Bhima's death-grip. He gasped for breath. When Keechaka's battered body became limp, Bhima began rolling it on the ground. Then he paused for a while and struck again fiercely at Keechaka's body, pounding it with his fists and stamping it with his feet till it became only a bleeding mass of flesh. He broke the glad news of Keechaka's death to Draupadi and returned hurriedly to his own apartments unnoticed by any one.

Draupadi rejoiced over the death of the villain who wanted to molest her. She woke up the guards and said, "My Gandharva husbands have slain Keechaka."

Thousands of guards came rushing with torches in their hands. Seeing Keechaka's pulped dead body, they were wonder-struck, they thought it could only be the work of a superhuman being. Some of Keechaka's friends, seeing Draupadi standing nearby, said to King Virata, "Keechaka has been killed because of Sairandhri. We shall burn her with him." Getting the king's permission, they caught hold of her violently and brought her and placed her upon the bier, and started towards the cremation ground. Draupadi shouted for help.

Hearing her sorrowful cries Bhima rose from his bed, disguised himself and rushed towards them. He went out of the palace by scaling the walls and reached the cremation ground with an uprooted tree in hand. Seeing him approaching like Death, people began to tremble and said to one another, "Here comes the powerful Gandharva. Let us release Sairandhri and run away." In no time Bhima killed hundreds of them and freed Draupadi. The citizens ran to the king and said, "Sairandhri is free and Keechaka's men have been slain. She is beautiful and will tempt others too. Men are indeed lustful. Do what you think is best."

Filled with fear, the king said to Queen Sudekshana, "When Sairandhri returns, order her to quit our Kingdom. I dare not tell her this directly for she is protected by Gandharvas." Draupadi returned to her apartments. There, the queen communicated to her Virata's words, "Sairandhri, the King is afraid of your Gandharva husbands. Please leave us alone and go wherever you wish." Sairandhri replied, "Let me stay for only thirteen days more here. Then my Gandharva husbands will come and take me away. They will be obliged to you for this favour." Her request was granted.

COWS STOLEN

Meanwhile, the spies of Duryodhana searched for the Pandavas in all possible places of hiding. After months of futile search, they reported to King Duryodhana that the Pandavas had probably perished. Then came the news that the powerful Keechaka had been killed in single combat by a Gandharva. Duryodhana wondered, "Time is running short. What shall we do?" Karna said, "Who knows what has happened to them? Perhaps wild beasts have eaten them up. They might have even died in some accident. Let us forget about them." The King of Trigartas, Susarma who had often been defeated in battles by Keechaka said, "If the Gandharva had really killed Keechaka, let us now attack the King of Matsya who is my enemy and also annex the Kingdom of Virata since he is now helpless." Karna supported the idea. They decided that Susarma should attack Matsya from the south and thus draw out the army of Virata to the south for defence. Duryodhana with the Kaurava army would then launch a surprise attack on Virata from the northern side, since it would be relatively undefended.

On the seventh day of the dark lunar fortnight, the Kaurava kings set out in two divisions to steal cattle from Virata as a ploy. It was the last day of the period of exile for the Pandavas. The cows of Virata were stolen. The poor cowherds, unable to protect their cows, ran to the court of the King. Approaching the King humbly, they said, "O King, the Trigartas are taking away thousands of our cows. Rescue them speedily so that they may not be lost." The King then collected a huge army consisting of elephants, horses, chariots and footmen and marched in pursuit of the enemies. Virata's brothers and his son Snakasha prepared themselves for the coming war. When the horses were being brought for the King's chariot, Virata said to his brother Satanika, "Kanka, Vallala, Tantripala and the vigorous Damagranthi will be able to help us. Give them chariots and armour." Then the Pandavas with the exception of Arjuna delightedly got into the chariots as commanded by the King.

The army left the city and proceeded towards the field. The fighting began. The Trigarta brothers were powerful fighters. If Keechaka had been alive he would have quickly routed their army. But without him the King found the enemy formidable. Susarma met Virata and a duel ensued between them. The battle field was covered with a thick blanket of dust rising from the ground. Susarma took the Matsya King captive. Virata's bow was broken into two. He had lost his chariot though he himself was alive. Susarma placed him in his chariot and drove away speedily. Seeing their King captured, the Matsyas fled in fear in different directions. Yudhishthira said, "Bhima, release him, so that he may not be a prisoner of his enemies." Bhima saw a tree near by and uprooted it. Yudhishthira smiled and said, "Please Bhima, do not do that. We must not be recognised. If you use this technique, you will at once be recognised. Fight like the others."

Bhima, with his brothers Nakula and Sahadeva, ascended the chariot and sped fast towards Susarma. Yudhishthira followed them. The four of them challenged Trigarta. Seeing the four warriors following them, Virata fought Susarma with renewed vigour in his chariot itself. Suddenly Bhima jumped into the chariot of Susarma. Holding Susarma by the neck, Bhima placed him in his chariot and brought him to Yudhishthira. Yudhishthira ordered Bhima to release Susarma saying that he had already become the slave of King Virata and needed no further punishment. Susarma went away from their presence, his face burning with shame. The enemy had been routed and the cattle had been recovered. Virata was highly pleased with the four Pandavas.

Virata was extremely happy and thankful to the Pandavas. He said "By your strength, I have been saved today. I am now crowned with victory. I shall make you all Kings of Matsyas. My riches are yours. Tell me how else I can repay you?"

Yudhishthira said," O King! I am glad that we have been of some help to you. You have sheltered us and this is just our way of showing you our gratitude." But the King was not satisfied. He said again, "Come, I shall install you as the King of all the Matsyas. I bow down to you. It is only because of your support that I am able to see my kingdom and children once again today." Yudhishthira spoke gently and asked the King to send messengers to the city announcing his victory. He also ordered arrangements to be made for the triumphal return of the King to his own capital. They spent a very happy night on the battle field. They decided to leave for the city after sunrise.

UTTARA - THE BOASTER

When King Virata had gone out in pursuit of Trigartas, Duryodhana with Bhishma and others attacked the kingdom from the northern side as had been planned. The Kaurava army marched in full force and rounded up the countless cattle that were there. The leader of the cowherds ran to the city and said to Prince Uttara, the son of Virata, "O Prince, the Kauravas are marching off robbing us of our cattle. King Virata has gone south to fight the Trigartas. We are in great confusion as there is no one to protect us. You are the prince, so we look to you for protection. At this critical hour you are engaged in playing Veena. Throw it aside and take up the Veena called the

bow, and play sweet music on the string of the bow and put fear into the hearts of your enemies with your music." When the leader of the cowherds made this complaint in the presence of the people, and especially of the women of the palace, the prince felt flushed with valour and proudly said, "If only I can get someone to be my charioteer, I shall vanquish the enemies and free the cattle. My charioteer was killed recently in the great encounter that had lasted for a month. I ask you all to get me a good charioteer immediately. I am not scared of the enemies. People who see me fighting will say, 'Is it Arjuna? There is no one else who can fight so well!' I am confident of that."

Draupadi was there listening to the words of Uttara. She ran to the princess and said, "Your brother says that he cannot fight because he has no suitable charioteer. I know of one who can help. Brihannala is a good charioteer. He was Arjuna's charioteer, when I was in the service of the Queen of the Pandavas, I also know that he has learnt archery from Arjuna. Order Brihannala to go and drive the chariot for Uttara."

The Princess was very happy. She ran to her brother and said, "I learn from Sairandhri that Brihannala is an expert charioteer and has served Arjuna. Take him. Go forth to save us and also cover yourself with glory."

ARJUNA FILLS UTTARA WITH COURAGE

The Prince agreed and at once the Princess ran to the dance hall and informed Brihannala that his services were required as charioteer. The Princess

arranged suitable battle gear for Brihannala. He pretended that he did not know how to put it on. He made such a fool of himself that all the girls in the hall laughed at him. The prince himself put the armour on Brihannala. He told Uttara, "I am ready, my Lord. I will take you wherever you want to go." Uttara said, "Go where the Kurus are. I am impatient to meet my enemies." Accordingly, Brihannala drove the chariot towards the Kurus. There they saw the enemy army arranged in battle array. Their huge division appeared like an ocean. Karna, Duryodhana and Bhishma were leading the Kuru army. Uttara's nerves failed him. He was in distress. He trembled and said to Brihannala, "I cannot do it, I simply cannot. Let me return. Let the Kauravas march off with the cows. I do not care. What sense is there in trying to fight people who are immeasurably stronger than me? Turn back the chariot or else I will jump out and walk back." Giving up honour and pride, he jumped out of the chariot and began to run towards the city in panic. Even as Uttara was running back Brihannala followed him and shouted at him to stop and behave like a Kshatriya, adding, "Even death is better than cowardice."

Uttara had not even taken a hundred steps when Brihannala caught up with him. Held by Brihannala, Uttara began to lament piteously and said, "O Brihannala, turn back the chariot. He who lives can hope to attain prosperity. I will give you one hundred coins of pure gold and many other things." Holding him forcibly, Brihannala said, "O Prince, if you do not like to fight with

your enemies, come, control the horses while I fight with them." Saying so, he took Uttara near the Sami tree and said, "Climb quickly. The weapons of the Pandavas are hidden on the topmost branches. Bring them down." "There is only a corpse hanging there. How can I, being a Prince, touch it with my own hands?" moaned Uttara. Brihannala said, "Fear not, there is no corpse. They are only weapons." Trembling, Uttara climbed up and brought down the bundle in which were the shining weapons. "Whose arms are these?" asked Uttara. Brihannala said, "This bow called Gandiva belongs to Arjuna. The sword is Bhima's. The other weapons belong to Yudhishthira, Nakula and Sahadeva." "But where are they? Where is Draupadi?" asked Uttara. Brihannala replied, "I am Arjuna. Your father's courtier is Yudhishthira. Bhima is a cook in your palace. Looking after the horses and the cows are Nakula and Sahadeva. Our wife Draupadi is the hair-dresser, Sairandhri." Uttara could not believe these words. He said, "I shall believe you if you can mention the ten names of Partha I have heard of." Arjuna laughed and said, "I shall tell you my ten names. Hear with attention. Arjuna, Phalguna, Jishnu, Kiriti, Swētavahana, Vibhatsu, Vijaya, Krishna, Savyasachi and Dhananjaya. I am called 'Arjuna' because I am white i.e. pūre in action and am of the complexion of the Arjuna tree. 'Phalguna,' because I was born on a day when the star Uttara Phalguna was in the ascendant; 'Jishnu,' because I am terrible when I am angry and I become unapproachable, irrepressible and dreadful. I am called 'Kiriti' because Indra placed a diadem, brilliant as the Sun on my head; 'Svetavahana' because only white horses draw my chariot in battles', 'Vijaya', because I always return victorious from battle; 'Krishna' because I was dark in complexion as a child. 'Savyasachi,' because I can shoot arrows with both hands and 'Dhananjaya,' because I conquered all the kings during the Rajasuya and collected wealth from all of them."

Uttara was satisfied. He approached Arjuna with respect and said, "Because of my good luck I have seen you. You should pardon me for what I had said out of my ignorance. I shall be your charioteer. Tell me where I should take you."

Arjuna said, "I am pleased with you. I shall destroy all your enemies. Tie all the quivers to the chariot and arm yourself with a golden sword."

COWS RECOVERED

The chariot of Arjuna thundered on its way as if it would shake the earth. Arjuna had now hoisted on his chariot the banner with the monkey symbol after removing the banner of the Matsyas. He twanged the bow Gandiva. The noise struck terror into the hearts of the Kaurava forces. Drona was thrilled to hear the sounds of the Gandiva and conch of the Devadatta. He anxiously said, "Here comes Arjuna. I know he will be a terror to our armies. Our armies must be arranged well and with care." Duryodhana did not like the way Drona praised Arjuna. He said, "The Pandavas' pledge was that they would spend twelve years in the forest and the following year unrecognized. The thirteenth year is not yet complete, but Arjuna has already come before that period.

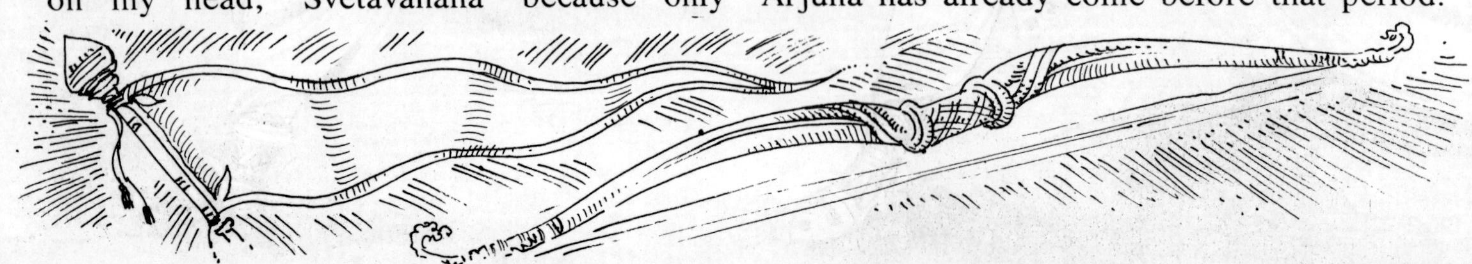

Therefore the Pandavas will have to pass another twelve years in the forest. It is proper that Bhishma calculates the exact number of years and tells us. At present we have to fight Arjuna. Bhishma, Drona and Kripa are just sitting quietly in their chariots, only because Arjuna has come. What if he has come? Can he put so much fear into our hearts? Should his presence frighten us? No, not at all. Arrange our armies in such a way that they do not break-up."

Karna said, pointing to the elders: "I see that all of you are looking as if terrified and panic-stricken and reluctant to fight. I shall fight alone. Today I shall redeem the promise I made to Duryodhana by killing Arjuna in battle." Thus as usual Karna began to brag. When Kripa heard these words of Karna, he said, "This is pure tomfoolery. If we are to win, we must all make a determined attack on Arjuna. Only then shall we win. Therefore do not brag about your opposing him unaided." Karna grew angry and said, "The Acharya always delights in glorifying Arjuna. Those who are afraid need not fight, but may simply look on while I fight." Aswatthama did not like Karna insulting the elders. He said, "The battle is yet to be won and the cows taken to Hastinapura but you are already bragging. In what battle did you heroes defeat the Pandavas? You dragged Draupadi to the assembly, and you are proud of it. A fight with Arjuna, you will find, is a different thing from the throw of a dice." The leaders of the Kaurava army became thoroughly impatient. Seeing this, Bhishma was filled with anguish and said, "The wise man does not insult his teachers. O Ashwatthama, do not take Karna's remarks seriously. This is not the time to nurse enmity or to sow dissension. Drona, Kripa and Aswatthama should forget and forgive. We can defeat Arjuna only if we all join together and fight him."

Bhishma then turned towards Duryodhana and said, "Your assumption is wrong, Arjuna has come after the stipulated period of thirteen years which ended yesterday. When I heard the sound of the twanging of the Gandiva, I understood that the period of your rule had ended and it was Arjuna that was coming for battle. Think before plunging into a fight with Arjuna. If you wish to make peace with the Pandavas, now is the opportune moment. What do you seek — a just and honourable peace or a mutually destructive war?" Duryodhana said, "I have no wish for peace, I shall not give even one village to the Pandavas. Let us get ready for war." Then Bhishma said, "Proceed quickly towards the city with one fourth of the army. Let another surround the cows and protect them. With the help of the remaining army, we shall fight Arjuna." Having sent away Duryodhana, Bhishma arranged his troops in battle array. Karna standing in the front, sent out a shower of arrows towards Arjuna. But Arjuna was ready to face single handed all the great heroes of the Kauravas. His arrows killed thousands. Drona was amazed at Arjuna's skill and the soldiers stood aghast at the terrible sight. Bhishma retreated, being pierced in ten places by Arjuna's shower of arrows. Arjuna said to Uttara, "I do not find Duryodhana. I am afraid he is retreating to save his own life. Just follow him quickly." Uttara, accordingly, drove the chariot towards Duryodhana.

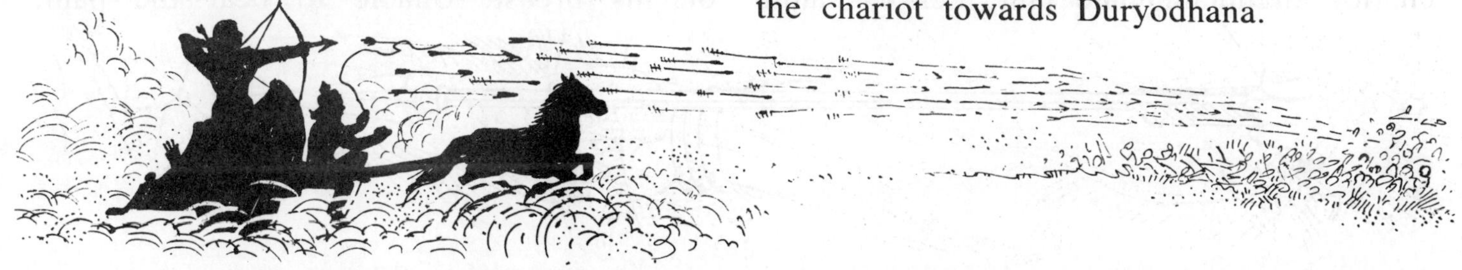

Kripacharya understanding Arjuna's intention said, "Arjuna wants to follow Duryodhana. Let us all attack Arjuna. None can fight him singly when he is angry. Of what use are cows or wealth if Duryodhana dies?" In the meantime, Arjuna, announcing his arrival, speedily showered arrows on the soldiers. The warriors could not see anything as the whole place became dark with arrows cast. They were so confused that they could not even run away. Instead, they stood wonder-struck and adored Arjuna. Arjuna blew the conch which made the hair of the enemies stand on end. He routed the enemies and recovered the cows. Then he proceeded towards Duryodhana.

ARJUNA HUMILIATES DURYODHANA.

On one side, Karna supported by powerful warriors, rushed towards Arjuna. From the other side, Bhishma, Drona and Kripacharya attacked him. A terrific battle took place between them. Karna taking advantage of it, wounded Arjuna's horse. But Arjuna was not deterred. With the help of the Gandiva, Arjuna severely wounded Karna who fled from the battle-field. After Karna's exit, the other heroes headed by Duryodhana shot arrows at Arjuna, just like the Sun covering the whole earth with its rays. The arrows shot from Arjuna's Gandiva filled the ten quarters. The enemies could see his chariot only when they came very close to them. The Kurus lost all their energy out of fear of Arjuna. He sent twelve arrows at Dusshasana and three at Kripa. Six arrows pierced Bhishma's body. Then he moved towards Drona. He said to Uttara, "Drona is very worthy of my reverence. Let the chariot circumambulate him. Let us salute him. I shall retaliate only if Drona strikes me first. Then he will not be angry."

Drona rushed towards Arjuna with great force. Arjuna was filled with joy and smiled. Saluting him, he said, "Sir, having completed our exile, we now wish to avenge the injustice meted out to us. Do not be angry with me. I will not strike you unless you strike me first. This is my pledge." Drona discharged several arrows at Arjuna, but Arjuna countered them all before they could fall on him. Both of them were equally skilled in warfare and well-versed in the use of celestial weapons. They spread a network of arrows. It was a fight between the Master and the Disciple. The other warriors shot a number of sharp arrows towards Arjuna's chariot. Arjuna, though wounded, speedily discharged similar arrows at Drona. Covered on all sides with deadly arrows, Drona looked like a mountain on fire. Then Aswatthama came to Drona's help. Though enraged, he was all praise for Arjuna. This gave Drona an opportunity to retreat. Then Arjuna had to encounter Aswatthama who, also unable to stand against him, retreated.

Seeing Karna come again, Arjuna shouted in anger, "O Karna, I give you another opportunity to keep up your boastful words uttered in the assembly, 'There is none equal to me in fight'." A great fight ensued between them. Karna rained arrows like a heavy downpour. Unable to bear the attack of Karna, Arjuna cut off the string of Karna's bow. This time Karna threw the arrows at Arjuna with his bare hands. Arjuna lost control of his bow. Still undeterred, Arjuna sent a powerful arrow which struck Karna on his breast. Unable to bear the pain,

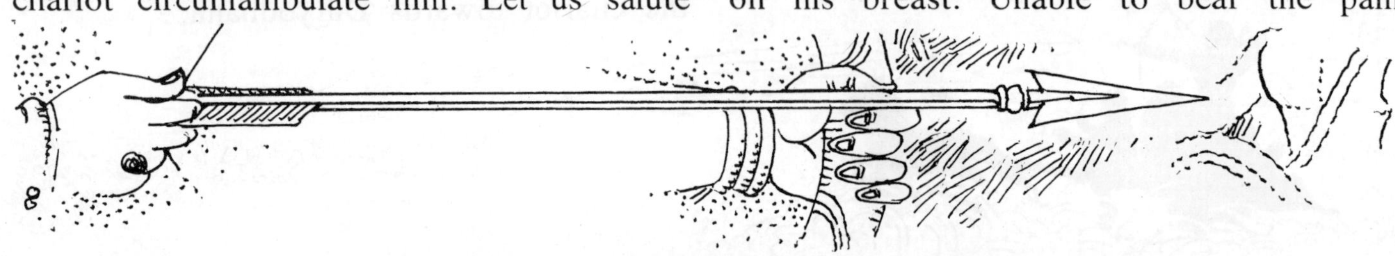

Karna once again fled from the battlefield. Arjuna and Uttara burst into laughter.

A snake-headed arrow from Duryodhana's fully stretched bow grazed Arjuna's forehead. But he stood firm, while blood trickled down his body. Angered, he fired a number of snake-arrows at Duryodhana, attacking him relentessly. Duryodhana started fleeing but soon retraced his steps on hearing the taunts of Arjuna and resumed the fight. Bhishma and others also came back and tried to protect him. Arjuna fought undauntingly and finally fired a magic weapon called 'Sammohana' which made them all fall unconscious. While. they were in that condition, he snatched away their garments. Recovering, Duryodhana asked Bhishma, "Why did you not shoot at Arjuna?" Bhishma smiled and replied sarcastically "I did not know that mere noise would paralyse you."

Arjuna said to Uttara, "Let us turn back. The cattle have been recovered and the enemy routed." Arjuna, on the way, said to Uttara, "It is known to you alone that we, the Pandavas, are living with your father. Keep it a secret, else your father will die of sheer fear. On entering the city you announce this as your own victory saying, 'The Kaurava army has been defeated and cows recovered!.'"

They came back to the cremation ground under the Sami tree. Hanuman flew away from the flag of Arjuna and it was replaced by a flag with the symbol of a lion. They put back the weapons on the tree in the same place as before. Arjuna asked Uttara to send messengers to Virata to announce in advance the news of their victory. Arjuna took the reins of the chariot from Uttara and entered the city as Brihannala.

PANDAVAS REVEAL THEIR IDENTITY

When the news of the victory reached Virata, Yudhishthira remarked, "As Brihannala was the charioteer, the enemy could not take away the cows." Virata ordered the courtiers and musicians to welcome his son to the city and sent his daughter to welcome her brother. Then he turned to Yudhishthira and said, "I am in a happy mood, let us play dice." Yudhishthira replied "We have heard that when one is in great joy one should not gamble. I do not wish to play with you today. Haven't you heard of the fate of Yudhishthira, who lost his kingdom and all his brothers? But if you order, I shall play." When Virata insisted, they started playing. While they played, Virata said, "My son has routed the Kauravas." Yudhishthira said "Hurrah! Was not Brihannala his charioteer?"

Enraged by this remark, Virata said to Yudhishthira, "What do you mean, you scoundrel? Does my son need the help of a eunuch to win a battle? For the sake of friendship, I forgive you this time. You must not repeat this offence again." Yudhishthira again said, "When Drona, Bhishma and others assemble to fight, who else can face them except Brihannala. None has been his equal and none will be his equal." Virata flung the dice at Yudhishthira and blood flowed from his nose. He held it quickly in his cupped hand so that it might not fall on the ground. Understanding his move, Sairandhri brought a golden jug of water and he poured the blood into it.

Meanwhile, Uttara entered the capital, applauded by crowds of citizens. He sent a messenger to the King, with the words, "Your son waits at the gate with Brihannala." The King said, "Bring them here. I am anxious to meet them. " But Yudhishthira whispered to the messenger, "Let Uttara come alone. Brihannala has taken a vow that whoever will inflict a wound on my body or shed my blood, except in battle, will not be allowed to live thereafter. Greatly angered on seeing me bleed, he will kill Virata." As Uttara entered, he noticed Yudhishthira's bleeding nose. and enquired of his father as to who was the cause for this. Virata said, "I did it because he praised the ennuch more than you." Uttara said, "You have committed a great sin. Ask for his forgiveness before he utters a deadly curse on us all." By the time Brihannala entered the bleeding stopped. He stood silent. Virata having pacified Yudhishthira praised Uttara in the hearing of Arjuna, "O Uttara, my son, your exploits give me much happiness. You freed the cows destroying the enemies." Uttara said, "I did not recover the cattle, Nor did I rout the Kauravas. Seeing me running away from the battlefield in fear, a person stopped me, mounted my chariot and slaughtered the enemy. And when the battle was won, he disappeared. But he will return either tomorrow or the day after or who knows when?"

On the third day, after a bath and clad in white, and wearing numerous ornaments, the Pandavas entered the hall and sat on the throne reserved for the kings. Virata, being angry with their behaviour shouted at Yudhishthira, "You Kanka, a dice player, how dare you sit on a royal throne?" Arjuna retorted, "Not merely on a king's throne, he is worthy of sitting on the throne of Indra, for he is Yudhishthira, son of Pandu." He then pointed out the other brothers by their names. Virata was wonderstruck to know their identities. He felt sad that he had engaged these honourable persons to do menial jobs. He immediately made an alliance with Yudhishthira and offered him the entire kingdom. He also offered his daughter Uttara to Arjuna. Yudhishthira glanced at Arjuna. But Arjuna replied, "I shall accept your daughter as my daughter-in-law. It would make a good alliance."

"Why should you not take her as your wife, Arjuna?" asked Virata. Arjuna replied, "While living in the women's quarters, I looked after her as my daughter and she respects me as her father."

Many kings from near and distant lands attended the marriage of Arjuna's son Abhimanyu and Uttara. Krishna came decked with garlands, accompanied by Balarama and other Vrishnis. Abhimanyu's marriage with Uttara was performed in a grand manner according to the Vedic rites in the august presense of Lord Krishna and illustrious kings and friends.

Thus ends Virata Parva.

UDYOGA PARVA

ARJUNA & DURYODHANA AT DWARAKA

After the wedding celebrations the Pandavas met in the assembly hall of Virata. Krishna sat next to Yudhishthira and Virata. When the proceedings of the assembly started, all eyes turned towards Krishna. He rose and said, "You all know how Yudhishthira was cheated by a trick at a game of dice and was deprived of his kingdom and was in exile with his brothers for thirteen years. Though they were capable of taking back their kingdom by force at any time, still they kept their word and lived in exile. For thirteen years, they suffered patiently. Consider this well, O Kings. A promise has been kept — the Pandavas have been truthful. The intentions of Duryodhana are not known to us. Therefore, let a worthy messenger be sent to him with a request to return Yudhishthira's kingdom."

Balarama then got up and said, "You have just heard Krishna. I endorse his proposition. War is not our objective but peace. Anything gained by peaceful means is really more beneficial than a thing gained by war" But Satyaki and Drupada were not for any message of peace to Duryodhana. They thought that there was no need for Yudhishthira to beg anything from Duryodhana. Nevertheless Krishna wanted an opportunity to be given to Duryodhana. He suggested that the following message be sent to Dhritarashtra.

"If the Kauravas want peace on the basis of equality of shares, we are ready for it; if not, we shall adopt other means."

Having decided thus, Krishna left for Dwaraka with his people. Then Drupada sent his priest to the Kauravas, while Duryodhana's spies brought him the news of the conference in Virata's court. Duryodhana began preparing for the ensuing war and sent word to his friends to ready their armies also. The Pandavas also sent word to kings who were likely to support their cause, to mobilize their forces to help them. Arjuna himself went to Dwaraka to seek the help of Krishna. Duryodhana too, having heard that Krishna had left for Dwaraka, went to seek his help. Both of them reached Dwaraka on the same day and found Krishna asleep. Duryodhana sat on a cushion near his head, but Arjuna stood with folded arms at Krishna's feet. When Krishna woke up, he first saw Arjuna and then Duryodhana. Krishna welcomed them both and asked what brought them to him. Duryodhana said, "O Krishna! It is befitting that you should help me in this war. You are a friend of both of us but, I have come before him seeking your help. Tradition has it that the first come is served first."

Krishna said, "Though you came first, my eyes fell first on Arjuna. I shall help both of you. The younger person is served first. Therefore, I should first offer my assistance to Arjuna. There is a large army of a hundred million gopas known as Narayanas who are capable of fighting in a battle. In my distribution of assistance they all will be on one side. As for me, I will not touch weapons or fight but will be on the other side. Arjuna, you select first. Do you want me alone, weaponless, or my army?"

When Krishna had finished, Arjuna said without any hesitation, "I choose you even though you may not fight." Duryodhana was very happy to get the large army of Krishna. He felt that without the army and weapons, Krishna could not be of much help. He thanked Krishna profusely and then went to Balarama for help. The mighty Balarama said, "Duryodhana, you must have heard what I told at the time of Abhimanyu's marriage. I spoke in favour of you. But now Krishna has aligned himself with the

Pandavas. I shall not help you or Arjuna as it is impossible for me to be separated from Krishna and fight against him. You are born in the illustrious family of the Kurus. Go and fight bravely in strict accordance with the rules of Dharma."

Duryodhana then went to Kritavarma, who gave him an army of one Akshauhini.

After the departure of Duryodhana, Krishna asked Arjuna, "Why did you choose me, even after knowing that I would not fight?" Arjuna answered, "There is no doubt that you can slay all of them. So too I alone can slay them all. In this world you are an eminent person and I shall attain the same state as you by killing them all single handed. So, I desired that I win the battle with you as my charioteer unarmed. This has been my desire for long and today you have kindly fulfilled my wish." Krishna was happy at Arjuna's confidence. He said, "I shall act as your charioteer, let your desire be fulfilled." Then both of them returned to Yudhishthira.

Hearing that King Shalya, brother of Madri was camping with his army in a nearby place, Duryodhana went to him, paid him homage and entertained him with the choicest meat and wines. Pleased, Shalya embraced Duryodhana, and said, "What can I do for you?." "I want you to be the leader of my armies," replied Duryodhana. Shalya reluctantly agreed. In fact he was on his way to meet the Pandavas to offer his help to them.

PEACE EFFORTS

When Drupada's priest arrived in Hastinapura, he was welcomed by Dhritarashtra, Drona and Bhishma. The priest of Drupada explained the purpose of his visit. He said, "O King! It is not for me to discuss the common lineage of the Kauravas and the Pandavas. I only suggest that the kingdom be equally divided between the Kauravas and the Pandavas. Dharma demands the return of what has been taken. An agreement must be honoured." Having heard him, Bhishma said, "We are happy that the Pandavas seek peace with the Kauravas. You are narrating the truth and you have stated the case well." While Bhishma was speaking, Karna angrily interrupted, "O Brahmin! What you say is known to everyone. There is no point in repeating the same thing. If the Pandavas think they can pressurize Duryodhana into giving up half the kingdom, they are mistaken. Since they were detected before the stipulated time, they must once again go back to the forest."

"Tall talk," said Bhishma, "Remember, Arjuna had vanquished the six Kaurava heroes in Virata's kingdom. If we do not listen to this Brahmana's plea, most certainly we will be killed by Arjuna." Dhritarashtra endorsed Bhishma's words and condemned Karna. He said to the Brahmin, "Go back to the Pandavas and tell them I shall think over this and decide what is best for all concerned. I shall send my response through Sanjaya."

Accordingly, the Brahmin returned. Then Dhritarashtra called Sanjaya aside and instructed him thus: "Sanjaya, go to the sons of Pandu and convey to them my affectionate regards. Enquire about their welfare. They have always been good and obedient. Naturally, they will like us. See that no hostile or war-like word escapes your lips. Use your discretion and be specially gentle to Krishna. They will do nothing unless he approves of it."

SANJAYA AS PEACE MESSENGER

Thus instructed by Dhritarashtra, Sanjaya went to Upaplavya where the Pandavas were camping. Sanjaya saluted Yudhishthira and said, "Dhritarashtra enquires about the health of all of you." Yudhishthira said, "O Sanjaya! We are delighted to meet you after a long time." "I bring a message from King Dhritarashtra" said Sanjaya, "And I would request you to listen to it carefully. He praises your righteousness and humility. He says you always know what is the right thing to be done. He knows that you consider an evil act to be a blot on the family honour, like a speck of dirt on a white sheet. On his behalf, I prostrate myself before Krishna and Drupada. I beg that you act in a way that will bring prosperity to the family."

Yudhishthira said, "It is very strange. What have I said that makes you believe that I desire war? Who does not know the dangers of war? You know the whole story of our relations with Duryodhana and others. We are still the same Pandavas. Friendship is still our hope. But, Indraprastha must be returned to us." "But why do you insist on this?" asked Sanjaya, "I consider living as a beggar better than attaining the kingdom by means of war. Anger is a vicious drug. It goes to the head and leads to ruin. Is not patience better?" Yudhishthira said, "Undoubtedly. But you should understand who is right and who is wrong. Here is Krishna. He desires the welfare of both the parties. Let him say if I am wrong. I shall act according to his advice."

Krishna said, "O Sanjaya! I wish happiness and prosperity for both the Kauravas and the Pandavas. Can you deny that Duryodhana wants the entire kingdom for himself? Do not think Sanjaya, that you know more about what is right and wrong than I or Yudhishthira. When the lustful Dusshasana dragged Draupadi into the assembly hall, none of the Kurus except Vidura uttered a word in protest. Duryodhana resembles a big tree, full of malice, Karna the trunk, Sakuni a branch. Dushasana represents its numerous fruits and flowers, with King Dhritarashtra forming the root. Whereas Yudhishthira is a big tree full of virtue, Arjuna the trunk and Bhimasena its branch. Nakula and Sahadeva represent the fruits and flowers, with myself the supreme Being and the Brahmanas the roots. I shall go

there personally and speak to them words of wisdom based on the principles of virtue and humility. I hope they will treat me with respect and listen to me. Otherwise Bhima and Arjuna will reply fittingly." Yudhishthira said to Sanjaya, "Sanjaya, go in peace, and on my behalf, tell Duryodhana to give me back my kingdom or prepare for war. Please pay my respects to Dhritarashtra and make kind enquiries of his health on my behalf and tell him this from me: 'Was it not through your generosity that we obtained a share of the kingdom when we were young? I hope you who made me a king once would not now deny us our share and force us to lead a beggar's life, living on the charity of others.' Convey my love and regards to Bhishma, Drona, Vidura and others."

DURYODHANA IS ADAMANT ON WAR

Sanjaya took leave of them all and left for Hastinapura. On reaching the palace, Sanjaya went to Dhritarashtra and said, "O King! Yudhishthira is well. He sends his respects to you all. By depriving him of his kingdom you will be bringing about the destruction of your race. You, being influenced by your headstrong son, regarded success as certain and did not prevent the game of dice. Now you will face its consequences. After a long journey, I am too tired today. Please permit me to rest. Tomorrow in the assembly, I shall convey the message of the Pandavas." After Sanjaya left, Dhritarashtra could not get a wink of sleep that night due to anxiety. He sent for Vidura and spent the whole night talking to him. Vidura said, "You say you don't get sleep. Sleep deserts a thief, a defeated man, a weakling, a lustful man, and a person who has lost his wealth having been attacked by a brave enemy. I trust none of these is applicable in your case. Have you coveted other's wealth?"

Next morning, the assembly was full. Everyone was eager to hear Sanjaya. Dhritarashtra said, "I command you Sanjaya to tell us exactly the message you have been given."

Sanjaya got up from his seat and said, "Let Duryodhana listen to Arjuna's message. Arjuna has said, 'If Duryodhana does not surrender the Kingdom, he will reap the consequences of his refusal. Krishna and I are going to destroy Duryodhana and his followers, root and all'."

After hearing the words of Sanjaya, the venerable Bhishma spoke to Duryodhana. He said, "My dear Duryodhana, you do not know the strength of Arjuna and Krishna. The sages say that they are Nara and Narayana. They are invincible. Give up your foolish thought of war with them. You are depending on three persons who advise you wrongly. They are the evil-minded Sakuni, the sinful Dusshasana and Karna who has been cursed by Bhargava."

These words of Bhishma did not please Duryodhana. Drona also spoke like Bhishma. "What Bhishma says is correct. Peace with the Pandavas seems to be the best option." Dhritarashtra asked Sanjaya to tell them more about the strength of the Pandavas Sanjaya narrated it graphically.

Dhritarashtra was frightened. He said, "When I listen to you, my heart trembles with fear for the lives of my sons. Bhima alone will destroy all my sons. I fear him as a deer fears a lion. I doubt whether I shall have any prosperity in the future. I foresee clearly the destruction of the Kauravas. The great calamity facing the Kauravas, beginning with the game of dice, now stands out clearly. Duryodhana, desiring riches, performed that wicked act. It is all my fate. I shall be helpless when I hear that my hundred sons have been killed and, at that time, I shall have to hear the loud wailing of women. Arjuna knows nothing but victory. Three forces have come together, I hear. They are Krishna, Arjuna and his Gandiva. I consider it will be wise on our part not to fight with them. If we wage war, the destruction of the Kauravas is certain. So, let us try for peace. Yudhishthira is a good man, we can deal personally with him."

Duryodhana who had been listening to all this got up and said, "Father, you need not be afraid of anybody. We know how strong we are. That we shall win is certain. Yudhishthira knows it too well. Giving up all hope of getting back the kingdom, he begs now for only five villages. Is it not clear from this that he is already frightened?"

Then Dhritarashtra wanted to know the strength of the Pandavas' army and the names of the kings who were supporting them. Sanjaya again narrated the size of the army as also the names of the great heroic kings who had already assembled in the city of Upaplavya. Hearing the description from Sanjaya, Dhritarashtra once again got frightened. He said, "I visualise in my mind's eye that all my foolish sons have ceased to exist already and along with Duryodhana the foolish kings who are supporting him have also been destroyed. I see death himself entering the bow Gandiva in order to destroy us. Disregarding my advice, Duryodhana desires to fight with those who are endowed with the power of righteousness and superhuman strength."

Duryodhana lost his temper and said, "My dear father, please do not lose confidence. Both sides are of the same race and both live on the same earth. Why then do you regard them to be superior?" Dhritarashtra was not impressed. He knew that what had been said by Sanjaya was true. So he said, "War is utterly detestable and dangerous. Half the kingdom is more than sufficient for you. Return the other half to the Pandavas. I know you will not normally behave thus. Bhishma, Drona and Sanjaya also feel that war should be avoided. Let us avoid war."

Duryodhana got quite wild and said, "Let nobody imagine that I am in need of anybody's half-hearted support. Bhishma and others can keep away if they so desire. Karna, Dusshasana and I alone will face the Pandavas. Either I shall rule this earth after killing the Pandavas or they will enjoy sovereignty over this earth after killing me. I can sacrifice my life, my kingdom, my wealth-indeed everything- but I shall not make peace with them. The Pandavas will not receive even a bit of land. That is certain. I am determined to fight it out now.''

Bhishma repeatedly advised Duryodhana to make peace with the Pandavas. But this good advice was not heeded by Duryodhana or his friends. They got up abruptly and walked away. In the excitement that prevailed, the court broke up. The hall was empty except for Dhritarashtra and his charioteer. Dhritarashtra sat there sorrowing.

WAR OR PEACE?

On the Pandava side, Yudhishthira too was worried. He did not want war. He said to Krishna, "Krishna, the time has come for a decision. You are our only refuge. Tell us what is good for us. For our sake, please go to Hastinapura and speak to Dhritarashtra. We have heard from Sanjaya what Dhritarashtra and his sons intend to do. We have lived for twelve years in the forest as ordered by him. But now he refuses to give back my kingdom. He doesn't care for Dharma or righteousness. I do not want war, I want only five villages so that I can live there with my brothers and Draupadi. In this predicament whom else can we consult but you, who are such a dear friend; who desires our welfare; who knows well the course of all actions and who is so well acquainted with the results of all actions."

Krishna said, "Yudhishthira, I shall certainly try to do what is best for both parties. If I succeed in my mission, mine will be the joy in having saved the world from destruction." Yudhishthira said, "I am afraid to send you there alone. You are our most precious possession. Duryodhana may try to harm you. If anything happens to you, even if we gain the whole world, we shall not be happy." Krishna smiled and said, "You are right. I know Duryodhana will speak ill of me and will try to harm me. Know that when I am angry, even if all the rulers of the earth join together they cannot stand before me any more than a group of small animals can stand before a lion. If they insult me I shall destroy the Kauravas. You have listened to Sanjaya. Do you still want to be friendly with the Kauravas? But the proper course for a Kshatriya is not to be so gentle and compassionate. A Kshatriya should welcome victory or death in battle. I am almost sure that Duryodhana will not part with the kingdom. So let all your armies be prepared for battle. It is to be taken for granted that on my return the war will have to be waged."

Bhima said, "O Krishna! If you can bring about a peaceful settlement I shall be very happy. At the same time do not frighten them with the prospects of a war. Duryodhana is by nature wicked. Speak no harsh words to him. I agree with my brother that there is nothing like peace. Try to convince our grandfather to avert war. I am sure my brother Arjuna agrees with me. He too is against war, if we can avoid it"

Lord Krishna was glad at heart to hear the words of Bhima. It was the last thing that he expected from Bhima. Coldness of fire or lightness of a mountain could be credible, but the soft-heartedness in Bhima was a surprise to Krishna. He said, "What is this I hear, Bhima? Till yesterday all of you were for war. During the last thirteen years, you did not have a single night of good sleep. You had no peace. You would sigh like an angry serpent and wring your hands in helpless fury against your brother who would ask you to be patient. You now talk of peace. Blaze up and yield not to grief. The dullness you show does not befit you."

Hearing the words of Krishna, Bhima replied, "Krishna, you have misunderstood me. Having known me for so many years, you should not call me a coward. I have strength enough to trample all the Kauravas under my feet. If you are not aware of my strength, you will see it in the battle to come. But now I don't want to spoil the chances of a peaceful settlement." Krishna smiled at him and said, "I know you, Bhima, well. It was out of deep affection I spoke to you. I wanted to rouse your spirit. I know that you are the strongest person on our side and that the Pandavas depend totally on you." Bhima was pacified.

Then Arjuna said, "Krishna, Yudhishthira has already told you everything. It is clear from your talk that you think peace is not possible. Yet I feel there is nothing that you cannot achieve. We shall accept with the utmost respect whatever you advise. I am not worried about the future. If you consider that the Kauravas are to be killed then let us have war immediately. Do whatever you think is best for us and the world. We are happy that you are with us, that is enough."

Krishna said, "Arjuna, you are right when you say that the will of God and human effort go together. But you are wrong in thinking that I can do anything with them. Do you think that without killing Duryodhana and others you will be able to get back your kingdom? The Kauravas are indeed doomed. I cannot work a miracle to save them. I shall try my utmost to avoid war, But don't hope very much for peace with the enemy. I shall convey to them what Yudhishthira has said."

'WITH MY RETURN, THE WAR WILL BEGIN'

Draupadi with her eyes filled with tears, the long black tresses untied, looked at Krishna and said, "O Krishna! you know how the Pandavas have been deprived us of the joys of life. My demand is that mercy should not be shown to the Kauravas in any way. They should be punished for their misdeeds. In doing so neither you nor the Pandavas will be touched by any sin. Which woman is there in this world equal to me? I was held by my hair in the presence of my husbands. I was treated like a common maid-servant and dragged in the assembly of those who are incarnations of evil. My husbands, the Pandavas, were mere spectators. It will be a shame on Arjuna's skill in archery and on Bhima's strength if Duryodhana is allowed to live. If you have mercy on me please aim for the destruction of the Kauravas."

She lifted her hair which looked like a big snake. She held it in her left hand and said 'Look at this hair which I have not combed since the day it was sullied by the hands of Dusshasana. Let all those who want peace, with the enemy look at this eternal reminder of shame and dishonour. If Bhima and Arjuna are so mean as to desire peace, then my father and my sons alone will fight the Kauravas. I have spent thirteen years waiting to take revenge on them."

The next moment Draupadi started crying, unable to control her grief.

Krishna comforted her saying, "Draupadi, the time is not far off when you will see the ladies in the inner apartments of Kauravas wailing and weeping on seeing their kinsmen and friends killed. I shall certainly accomplish this with the help of the Pandavas and I am sure that it is also the will of God."

The next day, preparations for Krishna's journey to Hastinapura began. He said to Satyaki, "Make my chariot ready, along with my conch, discus and mace. Duryodhana is a wicked person, so are Karna and Sakuni. Even a weak enemy should not be thought of lightly by strong men." Yudhishthira and the others led him to the chariot. Krishna took leave of them all. Accompanied by Satyaki, Krishna proceeded towards Hastinapura.

RECEPTION TO LORD KRISHNA

Dhritarashtra received advance information of Krishna's mission from his spies. He immediately summoned Bhishma, Drona, Vidura, Sanjaya and Duryodhana. He said to them, "The great Krishna is coming here on a mission on behalf of the Pandavas. On him depends the course of the world. He is coming here to talk about peace and war. He must be properly honoured. We must please him in every way and make his stay comfortable. His goodwill is necessary for us. If we please him, he will support us. Order the citizens to receive him with the warmest welcome. Let flags and banners flutter on all the towers, let the roadside be cleaned and watered." Bhishma and others approved of his suggestions. Duryodhana made all arrangements. Dhritarashtra said to Vidura, "Krishna will halt at Kasasthala tonight and arrive in Hastinapura tomorrow. I shall honour him with presents of gems and other costly gifts. I am eager to please him."

Vidura said, "Krishna is the greatest man ever born on this earth. He deserves all the honours you speak of and even more. But that is not the point. I have known you from your childhood. You are devising methods by which you can bribe that great person. You want to draw him to your side. How is it that suddenly you have become so generous? You have not the heart to part with even five villages to the Pandavas. I am sure he will not cast his eyes on anything but only a pot full of water to wash his feet. The Pandavas are also your children. Why not show them that love and affection a father ought to show his children?"

Duryodhana who was listening said, "What Vidura has said about Krishna is very correct. He is deeply attached to the Pandavas. No gifts should be wasted on him. He will think that we are honouring him out of fear." Bhishma said, "It is immaterial to Krishna whether you honour him or not. He is coming here for righting the wrongs done to the Pandavas. He will be pleased if we seek peace with the Pandavas with his help." At these words, Duryodhana became angry and said, "Listen to my plan, Grandfather. I will imprison Krishna here. Without Krishna, what can the Pandavas do?"

Dhritarashtra was horrified at this suggestion. He said, "It is against virtue to arrest an envoy on a peace mission. Moreover, he has done nothing wrong to us." Then Bhishma said, "Duryodhana can think only in an evil manner. Instead of listening to our advice, you too follow him. I don't wish to stay here any longer." Saying thus Bhishma left the assembly hall.

In the morning, Krishna arrived at Hastinapura. Dhritarashtra, accompanied by Bhishma, Drona and Kripa went to welcome him. All the citizens came out to have darshan of Lord Krishna. Krishna then entered the palace of the King. He greeted the elders respectfully and after the formalities of reception were over, he went along with Vidura to his house. Kunti was staying with Vidura. She greeted him in a voice choked with emotion. She enquired about the welfare of the Pandavas. Krishna told her how the Pandavas had lived through the years of exile and how they constantly remembered and chanted her name. He said, "The Pandavas along with Draupadi send their salutations to you. You will meet the Pandavas soon. They will become prosperous once again. Happy days are ahead for you and your children."

KRISHNA GLADDENS VIDURA

Krishna then went to the palace of Duryodhana. It was like the palace of Indra, furnished with various kinds of gems, and precious stones. Duryodhana was sitting on a throne. Karna, Dusshasana and Sakuni were sitting by his side. All of them stood up and greeted Krishna cordially. A special seat studded with precious stones and inlaid with ivory and gold was reserved for Krishna. Krishna sat on it with a smile.

Duryodhana said, "We had arranged a dinner for you and also made arrangements for your comfortable stay. But you decided to be the guest of Vidura. What is the reason?" Krishna said, "Duryodhana, I am very much satisfied with your welcome. Now I have come here as a mediator and I shall definitely be your guest when my work is finished." Duryodhana said, " That is beside the point. You may have come here as an envoy, but you are related to us. There is no enmity between you and me. We are very fond of you."

Then Krishna said frankly, "I did not want to be your guest, because I do not relish food in the house of an unrighteous person. You have been hating the Pandavas for the last so many years without any just cause. They are very dear to me. One who is a slave to avarice and ill-treats others is unworthy of my recognition. Whoever hates the Pandavas hates me as well because I am firmly allied with the Pandavas." Saying so he got up and walked towards the house of Vidura. Kripa and Bhishma followed him. They requested him to be their guest. But Krishna preferred to stay with Vidura. Vidura was in an ecstasy of joy. He attended to Krishna's wants with the utmost devotion and solicitude.

At night Krishna and Vidura had a conversation. Vidura said, "Lord, you should not have come on this mission of peace. Duryodhana is a fool and will not listen to anybody's advice. He is bent on war. He thinks that he can win the war with the help of Bhishma, Drona, Kripa, Ashwathama, Karna and Jayadratha. Puffed up with pride over the great army he has mobilized, he thinks that victory is already his. He is of the firm conviction that Karna can singly destroy all his enemies. So there is no meaning in talking about peace. In fact, I don't want you to go there, for

they may even insult you, and when that happens how can I be a silent spectator?"

Lord Krishna said, "What you say is doubtlessly true. However, my reason for coming here is this. I only wish to try rescuing these people from the death which is imminent. I will achieve great fame if I succeed in this. With all sincerity I shall try for peace. The hour of death has come upon the house of the Kurus. If, even after knowing that, I do not try to prevent it, then I am not their friend. I am keen on doing this service to the Kauravas. Moreover, I am very fond of Yudhishthira. He is the greatest man born on this earth. He loves peace. It is an honour to oblige him in trying for peace. This is the reason for my coming here." Thus talking the two wise men spent the night.

KRISHNA AT ASSEMBLY HALL

In the morning, Krishna accompanied by Vidura came to the assembly hall. Dhritarashtra and the entire assembly got up from their seats and honoured Sri Krishna. Narada and other Rishis were in the assembly to watch the proceedings. The whole assembly looked intently at Krishna.

His charming eyes lent brilliance to the great hall. With his favourite jewel Kaustubha glittering on his chest, and the famous yellow silk draping his dark body, Krishna looked like a blue mountain lit up by the yellow rays of the rising sun. There was absolute silence in the hall.

Krishna looked at Dhritarashtra and said, "I have come here to prevent the death of so many heroes. I have nothing new to say now. You know everything. The house of the Kurus is the best among all the races. It is famous for kindness, sympathy, truthfulness, generosity and

love of justice. But your sons want to deceive the Pandavas. If you don't correct them, the whole world will be destroyed. If you really so wish you can control them and ask them to make peace with the Pandavas. I advise you to do so in the interest of all. If you have a strong will you can achieve it. Be firm with your sons and establish your authority. Both the Kauravas and the Pandavas will be saved if you intervene and do something." Everyone listened to him attentively.

Following him, Parasurama, Kanwa, Narada and other great sages also advised Dhritarashtra and Duryodhana to make peace with the Pandavas for their own good. Finding that everyone was for peace, Dhritarashtra at last said to Lord Krishna, "Krishna, your words are noble and reasonable. But do you not see how helpless I am? Don't you see what my son's attitude is? If you can persuade him, I shall be very happy. He does not listen to words of sound advice from anyone. His mother Gandhari, Vidura and Bhishma have all tried to persuade him to change his attitude. But all in vain. If you can succeed where others have failed, I shall be extremely happy."

Krishna turned to Duryodhana and said, "Listen to me carefully Duryodhana, for your own good. You are learned and intelligent. Why then do you behave thus? Your obstinacy is dangerous to your own well-being. There will be frightful destruction if war begins. Make peace with the Pandavas. Peace will be to your own benefit as also to that of the entire world. In a crisis it is always safe to follow one's father's advice. There are three kinds of people in this world. The first type of persons are righteous by nature. The second one consists of people who consider only their own selfish interests. Even if you are of the second type, it is profitable to make

peace with the Pandavas. The third type of people delight in doing only what is wrong by listening to the advice of vicious friends. Don't come under the third type. You have already done enough injustice to the Pandavas. Still they are magnanimous and are ready to forgive and forget."

When Krishna had finished speaking, Bhishma found that Krishna's appeal had still made no impact on Duryodhana. Then he said, "My child, be not obstinate. Heed the appeal of Krishna. It will bring you prosperity. Otherwise you will perish and also bring about the destruction of the whole Bharata race even while your father is alive."

Drona also appealed to Duryodhana. He said, "O Duryodhana, Krishna's words are conducive to your happiness. Heed his appeal." Then Vidura said, "Duryodhana, I am not at all sorry for you, I am only sorry for Gandhari and Dhritarashtra. The time is not far off when they would have to wander forlorn and helpless. They will be friendless and miserable in this wide world."

DURYODHANA DEFENDS HIMSELF

Duryodhana was listening silently to all these appeals. At last, he turned towards Krishna and said, "Krishna, you always find fault with me. Now, even Bhishma and my father are joining hands with you in criticising me. What wrong have I done to deserve all this blame? Let me relate to you all that has happened so far. Yudhishthira willingly played the game of dice with my uncle and lost his kingdom to him. Why do you blame me for that? However, on my father's advice, I returned his kingdom. But they played again and lost. Am I to be blamed for that? They lost the game and went to the forest and now, they have mobilised an army in alliance with the Panchalas and are trying to pick up a quarrel with me. By their words and actions, they want to threaten me. Being a Kshatriya, I shall not yield to threats even if Indra challenges me. There are none who are strong enough to defeat us in battle, when I have Bhishma, Kripa, Drona and Karna on my side. I am only following the duty of a Kshatriya in preparing to fight with those who are picking up quarrels unnecessarily with me. It is better to die in battle like a hero and attain heaven than to surrender to my enemy. I have always lived like a king. I shall bow down only to my elders out of respect and not to the enemy out of fear. As far as the kingdom is concerned, no doubt Indraprastha was given to them by my father. I am aware of it. At that time, I was too young and dependent on others. It was given out of sheer ignorance and fear. But now I shall not allow it to be returned to them. Not even land measuring a needle's point will be surrendered to the Pandavas. Know this to be my final decision."

Krishna understood the anger of Duryodhana. He laughed and said, "Duryodhana, you think you should not be blamed for the recent happenings. Let the elders decide for themselves whether your words are true or false. Without consulting any of the elders you arranged the infamous game of dice. You played this game only with the intention of depriving the Pandavas of their kingdom. Yet, you say that you never harmed them. Look at Draupadi. All the Kurus have not yet forgotten how she was humiliated in the assembly by you and your brothers. You have been advised repeatedly by your mother, father, Bhishma, Drona and Vidura to make peace with the Pandavas. But, you never heeded their advice. Is this honouring your elders?"

Hearing Krishna's words, Dusshasana got up and said, "O Brother! It seems to me that if you do not agree to make peace, your own people will bind you hand and foot and hand you over to the Pandavas. Let us get away from here." Duryodhana accompained by his brothers walked out of the court angrily.

Krishna looked at all of them and said, "I blame all of you who have assembled here. For the good of the family, you should have kept this sinner long ago under strict control. At least now bind these four men Duryodhana, Dusshasana, Karna and Sakuni and hand them over to the Pandavas. I hope you will listen to me and act accordingly."

Hearing these angry words of Krishna, Dhritarashtra turned to Vidura, and said "Go and bring Gandhari to the court. With her help I shall try to bring Duryodhana to his senses." When Gandhari came, Duryodhana returned to the court his eyes red with anger. Gandhari tried repeatedly to bring him around to listen to his father. Duryodhana said, "No", and again walked out of the hall. He went straight to Karna, Sakuni and Dusshasana to consult them about their future plan of action. Dusshasana said, "I am sure they are planning to capture us and hand us over to the Pandavas. Dhritarashtra will be helpless." Duryodhana sighed with impatience. They conferred for a while and then Duryodhana said, "Krishna wants us to be taken captive. Instead we shall take him captive. Hearing that he has been captured, the Pandavas will then lose heart and we can tackle them easily Let us hurry and do it."

THE GRAND FORM OF SRI KRISHNA

The intelligent Satyaki had already anticipated their move. He hurried to Kritavarma and said, "Duryodhana and his friends are planning to capture Krishna. Go and call out our army quickly. Meanwhile, I shall inform Krishna of their plot." Satyaki rushed to the hall and broke the news to Krishna, Dhritarashtra and the others present. Vidura was horrified. Krishna was not perturbed. He smiled and pacified Vidura and said, "Be not afraid, it is not so easy to capture me. Since they persist in their wickedness, Yudhishthira has all the greater chances of success."

Hearing this, Dhritarashtra said to Vidura, "Bring the wicked Duryodhana along with his friends to me." When Duryodhana came, Dhritarashtra rebuked him, "How utterly mad is your plan of taking Krishna captive. Your effort is like that of a child trying to catch the moon with his tiny hands!" Krishna laughed at Duryodhana and said, "Duryodhana, you are a fool. You think that I am alone and that you can capture me. Open your eyes and look at me. The Pandavas, the Andhakas and the Vrishnis; the twelve suns and the eleven Rudras, the eight Vasus and great sages are all in my body. You can see all of them."

Saying thus Krishna laughed aloud. With his laughter, the body of Krishna began to glow. All the Devas could be seen emerging out of his body. He now assumed a terrifying form. The gods looked smaller than the thumb of his hand. On his forehead could be seen Brahma, the creator. On his huge chest could be seen Rudra. The supporters of the universe were seated on his arms. Agni could be seen glowing from his mouth. The twelve Adityas, Vasus and Ashwinis, the Maruts and all the Gods of heaven were visible on his body. Perched on his left hand could be seen the heroic kings and Arjuna with his Gandiva was seated on his right hand. Behind him were Bhima, Nakula, Sahadeva and Yudhishthira. The heroes of Vrishni and Andhaka were standing by his side. In front of Krishna were the other chiefs with their arms upraised. Fire could be seen flaming out of his eyes, ears and nostrils.

The Kings were bewildered to see this terrible aspect of Krishna. They closed their eyes in fear. Only Bhishma, Drona, Vidura and other great Rishis gazed at him with wonder and devotion. Lord Krishna gave them celestial vision to witness this rare phenomenon. Then a miracle happened, Krishna gave sight even to blind Dhritarashtra to see his 'Vishwarupa.' Flowers rained incessantly from the heavens on Krishna's head. Celestial drums were sounded. Dhritarashtra said, "You are bestower of good to the world. Please bless me, I have been able to see you. Having seen you, I do not want to see anything else. Please take away the power of sight from me. I do not want it." Krishna granted it. At that moment the earth shook, the waters of the ocean were agitated and the assembled kings stood struck with great wonder.

Then Krishna withdrew his Vishwarupa and assumed his original form. He took Satyaki and Vidura by the hand and went out of the hall. The Rishis led by Narada also departed. Krishna got into his chariot and left the palace. Then he met Kunti at Vidura's house. He narrated to her all that had taken place in the assembly. He said, "I have to go back now; let me take leave of you. Have you any message for the Pandavas?"

Kunti said, "Tell my sons that they are Kshatriyas and great heroes. They are the sons of Kunti. I expect them to behave like brave Kshatriyas. Give my greetings to Draupadi."

'KUNTI IS YOUR MOTHER'

Krishna took leave of Kunti and left for Upaplavya. While leaving he asked Karna to ascend his chariot. After travelling a short distance, Krishna said to Karna, "Karna, you are a good man. You have studied the Vedas. You are a son born to a virgin, but you know that the scriptures say that such a son must accept as father any man who has married his virgin mother. Your mother is Kunti and so you are Pandu's son, his eldest son, born before Yudhishthira. If I reveal this to the Pandavas, they will fall at your feet and give you all the respect you deserve."

Karna smiled and said, "I know I am morally Pandu's son. I also know that I am born to the Sun. But, my mother cast me away as soon as I was born, unconcerned about my welfare. It is Athiratha and Radha who gave me parental love and affection. I shall ever consider them as my parents. I shall not break my relationship with them even if I am offered the entire earth, heaps

of gold or any other worldly pleasures. No, Krishna, I cannot now turn my back on them. Moreover, I owe everything to Duryodhana. It is because of him that I enjoy sovereignty even though the world ostracizes me as a Sutaputra. I have fought Arjuna in single combat. But, I pray you don't disclose my identity to anybody. If Yudhishthira knows I am his elder brother, he will surrender the whole kingdom to me and will not fight. I know I used very harsh words to the Pandavas. I am sorry for it, but it is my duty now to do whatever Duryodhana bids me do."

Krishna then said, "Karna, it will be the end of the world if you do not heed my advice." Karna said, "If I am alive after this battle I shall meet you on earth or we will meet in Heaven." Saying this Karna embraced Krishna warmly and dismounted from the chariot and took leave of him.

As the objective of Krishna's visit had not been achieved, he returned to Upaplavya.

Meanwhile, Vidura went to Kunti and said, "Sleep has deserted me. The King is blind with pride, and Duryodhana will not listen; and the Pandavas are preparing for war." Kunti sighed deeply and said "Oh, what use is wealth when kinsmen perish?"

'YOU WILL HAVE FIVE SONS LIVING'

Kunti went to the banks of the Ganga where Karna usually offered his daily prayers. On the banks of Ganga, she heard the chanting of the Vedas by her son, a man of compassion and truth. She quiety stood behind him and waited. He was in meditation and was unmindful of everything until he felt the rays of the sun striking his back. His prayers over, he turned back only to find Kunti standing behind him and holding the hem of his upper garment over her head to shield it from the burning sun. The proud and powerful Karna smiled as if surprised and spoke to Kunti, "I am Karna, son of Radha and Athiratha. I bow to you. Pray, tell me what I can do for you."

Kunti replied, "You are Kunti's son and not Radha's. And Athiratha is not your father. You are not a Suta. Believe me. I was unmarried when I conceived you. You are my first son. You were born in Kuntiraja's palace. O Karna, you are the finest of fighters. God Surya is your father. Your birth is divine, my son. You were born with earrings and were clad in a

skin-coat of mail. Because you are not aware of it and are unable to recognise your brothers you are serving Duryodhana. Dharma requires one to please his parents. The kingdom of Yudhishthira has been usurped by Duryodhana. Recover it from his hands and enjoy it yourself. Today let the world see that Karna and Arjuna are brothers and that the brothers have reconciled. If Karna and Arjuna join together like Balarama and Krishna what is there that cannot be achieved in this world? You are my eldest son. Don't say you are a Suta's son. You are the radiant son of Kunti."

Then Karna heard an endearing voice issue from the solar disc speaking with the affection of a father. "Kunti speaks the truth. Follow your mother's advice, then you will be greatly benefited."

But neither the words of Kunti nor the voice of his father swayed Karna from his resolve. Karna said, "Mother, I do not respect the words spoken by you. The way you behaved with me when I was born was wholly unpardonable. I was born a Kshatriya but I was deprived of Kshatriya rights because of you. Could an enemy behave worse than this? When I required mercy, you showed none. You deprived me of my Samskaras. Now you come to me and make a show of love because you are in need of me. Who is not afraid of the alliance of Arjuna and Krishna? If I defect to the side of the Pandavas now, will they not say I am doing so out of fear? The sons of Dhritarashtra have accepted me. All my desires were granted and I was worshipped by them. I was happy and comfortable. They have now declared war. They need my help and they respect me as the Vasus respect Indra. They think that with my help, they can overcome their enemies. How can I go against their cherished desire? Even at the risk of my life, I must serve them to the end. I shall speak the truth to you. I shall be on the side of Duryodhana and fight with your sons with all my might. However, I don't want to disappoint you. I will honour your feelings. I promise you that I shall not kill any of your sons whom I can easily kill I mean Yudhishthira, Bhima and the twins except Arjuna. In Yudhishthira's army Arjuna alone is my equal. Either I will kill Arjuna or he will kill me and that will be a glorious end. In either case, you will have five sons living."

Kunti heard these words of Karna and trembled with fear. She embraced her son and said, "Destiny is the most powerful. What you say may come true. The Kurus will meet with destruction. Remember your promise and spare four Pandavas when missiles fly from your bow." She blessed him saying "May you prosper, my son." Then they parted.

WAR PREPARATIONS

Lord Krishna reached Upaplavya and told the Pandavas all that had happened at Hastinapura. He said, "I spoke urging what was right and also what was good for them. But it was all to no purpose. Now there is no way except war. The foolish Duryodhana would not listen to the advice of anybody. We must now prepare for war without wasting any time."

The Pandavas, in consultation with Krishna, selected Dhristadyumna as the commander of their army and moved towards Kurukshetra.

Draupadi and all other women folk remained at Upaplavya. The Pandavas camped on that part of Kurukshetra which was flat, pleasant and convenient for fodder and fuel supplies. After a night's rest the army moved again.

They reached the banks of the holy river Hiranvati which flows through Kurukshetra. Here Lord Krishna ordered a moat to be dug. Several tents were pitched. Hundreds of artisans, doctors and surgeons came there. Each tent had an attached hill-shaped armoury, stacked with bows and arrows, breast plates, battle axes; spears, swords, quivers, shafts and other weapons.

On the side of the Kauravas, Duryodhana approached Bhishma. He stood in front of him with folded hands and said, "Without a proper leader, even a powerful army is broken up in war. So without you we are helpless."

Bhishma said, "My child, I am quite willing to do as you wish. But the Pandavas too are as dear to me as you are. In fulfilment of my promise, I shall lead your army and perform my duty. Everyday I shall kill ten thousand warriors, but I shall not kill the Pandavas. One thing more, I will not fight if Karna fights on our side. He and I do not get on well with each other"

Duryodhana was in a dilemma. Immediately, Karna intervened and said, "I will keep off from the battle as long as Bhishma is alive. Only after Bhishma is slain, will I enter the battlefield."

Duryodhana appointed Bhishma as the commander-in-chief of the Kaurava army Drums and conchs were then sounded to announce the commencement of the war. The whole army led by Bhishma rolled on to Kurukshetra like a great flood.

The Pandavas heard about the selection of Bhishma as commander-in-chief. Yudhishthira told his seven army commanders to be alert. Arjuna was made the chief fighter. Krishna took up the reins of Arjuna's chariot. The soldiers shouted slogans; drums roared; and conchs blew in tens of thousands. thousands.

Balarama, Krishna's brother came to Yudhishthira accompanied by many members of the Vrishni race. Yudhishthira and his brothers gave him a warm welcome. They all greeted him and respectfully prostrated before him. Balarama said, "I hear a great war is to be fought. All the kings will be massacred mercilessly in it. I hope to see you all come out of the battle unharmed. It is clear that the war is now unavoidable. I have repeatedly told Krishna not to be partial towards either of the two parties. All of you are of one family and tied by blood to us. I have suggested to him to avoid the charge of favouritism. But he has refused to listen to my words out of his deep concern for you. Definitely, victory will be yours with Krishna holding the reins of Arjuna's chariot. None can dream of winning against Krishna. Bhima is very dear to me. I have however the same affection for Duryodhana also. Therefore, I have decided to go on a pilgrimage to the sacred places on the banks of Saraswati. If I remain here, I shall not be able to look on with indifference at the massacre of the Kurus." Balarama took leave of Krishna and others and went on a pilgrimage to holy places.

There came to the Pandavas, the great Rukmi, the king of Bhojakata. He was the brother of Rukmini, wife of Krishna. He had brought with him an army which numbered one Akshauhini. Yudhishthira received him cordially. Rukmi said, "Arjuna, you seem nervous on the eve of the war. I shall give you assistance. There is none in this world who is equal to me in strength. I shall destroy your enemies in the battle including Drona, Kripa and Bhishma." Rukmi looked at everyone and smiled to himself in smug self-confidence.

Arjuna then said, "Listen to me Rukmi. How can I say that I am afraid especially having Gandiva on my hand. We are not in need of your help. You may either go or stay on, just as you like." At this Rukmi was filled with anger and shame and went to Duryodhana's camp with his army. He said to Duryodhana, "The Pandavas have refused my help. My forces are at your disposal.' But Duryodhana also refused his help. Thus two persons, Balarama and Rukmi took no part in the great Kurukshetra war.

ULUKA AS A MESSENGER

The river Hiranvati became the line of demarcation between the two sides. Duryodhana discussed his plans with his associates and summoned Uluka, the son of Sakuni and told him, "Go at once to the Pandava camp and tell Yudhishthira in the midst of everyone. 'We are aware of your braggart message to us. Remember the vow you took in the assembly fourteen years ago. The time has come when you have to redeem your vow. I shall also give individual messages to his brothers and to Krishna. Bring me their answers to my messages' "

Uluka reached the Pandava camp. He repeated the words of Duryodhana which angered the Pandavas. They were so furious, they did not know what they could say in answer to the arrogant message of Duryodhana. They would have killed the messenger himself, but that would have been wrong. They therefore sent a message in reply, "Brave warriors do not repeat their vows. Instead they would redeem them by their action." Receiving their reply, Uluka returned to Duryodhana. Duryodhana assembled his army on the field of Kurukshetra ready to start the historic war. On the other side, Yudhisthira too moved his army, under the leadership of Dhrishtadyumna. It was a night full of anxiety and excitement for both the sides.

Bhishma, accepting the leadership of the Kaurava army, conferred with Duryodhana on the war plan he had made. He inspired Duryodhana by his own heroic spirit and cheerful self-confidence. In their discussion Karna became one of the subjects of talk. Bhishma said, "Karna has become your guide, friend and adviser. He is neither a Ratha nor an Atiratha in battle. The curse of Parasurama is on him. And the battle that will ensue between him and Arjuna will prove fatal for Karna. He brags a lot but quite often we see him retracing his steps." Drona too joined Bhishma in belittling Karna. Enraged by their harsh words Karna turned to Bhishma and made a bold and violent attack on him. He said, "O Grandsire, you are always seeking to humiliate me. You are literally envious of me. You seem to hate me, without limit or reason. I tolerate all this out of my concern for Duryodhana. You feel that I shall be of no use in the ensuing battle.

That is because you have least interest in the Kauravas Let me tell you my firm opinion of you. It is you not I — who will fail to be of use to the Kauravas, Hating me, you seek to come between me and Duryodhana. You try to poison his mind against me." Turning then to Duryodhana, Karna continued, "O King, age must be respected and the experience of elders will be certainly useful; but there is a point at which, the Shastras warn us, senility creeps in, making old men useless. You have made Bhishma the Supreme Commander. He will earn fame, from the heroic deeds of others. I shall not fight as long as Bhishma is alive. But after he has fallen I will fight."

Bhishma controlled his anger and said, "O Karna, as we are in a crisis I am sparing your life, or else you would have been the first person to be killed by me."

Duryodhana was in a predicament. He tried to console Bhishma. He said, "O Grandsire, I need the help of both of you. I am certain that both of you are great warriors. At the break of dawn, the battle will begin. Let there be no bickerings therefore at this critical moment." Duryodhana then asked Bhishma to narrate to him the strength and weaknesses of the Pandava side. Bhishma then described the strength and weakness of every hero on the Pandava side.

THE ONLY ENEMY OF BHISHMA

While mentioning the strength of great warriors Bhishma said, "Shikhandin, the son of Panchalas, is one of the foremost heroes on the Pandava side. He will do great deeds in the battle. But I shall not slay him even if he advances towards me ready to strike."

Duryodhana was quite astonished to hear this. He asked, "Why? You said you will slay the Panchalas. Why, then will you not kill their prince?"

Bhishma said, "It is a long story. Listen to my account. Then you will understand."

Bhishma continued, "Chitrangada and Vichitravirya were my brothers. After the death of Chitrangada, I installed Vichitravirya as the monarch. The virtuous Vichitravirya looked up to me in everything. I was thinking of getting him duly married. At that time news came that the daughters of the King of Kashi would be given in marriage at a Swayamvara. Their names were Amba, Ambalika and Ambika. Amba was the eldest of them. On behalf of Vichitravirya I attended the Swayamvara. Then, as was the custom, I challenged all the kings assembled there and forcibly took away the brides in my chariot. I said to them, "I, Bhishma, son of Shantanu, am taking these young women away by force in your very presence. O rulers of the earth, try with all your might to liberate them." Then a great war took place. They surrounded me on all sides with large troops of chariots. But I was too powerful. With a shower of arrows I arrested their rush easily and defeated every one of them. Unable to withstand my power, they turned back and withdrew. On the way Shalya attacked me again. But I humbled him too and returned to Hastinapura. Preparations for Vichitravirya's wedding were made. The wedding day was fixed but Amba said to me, "O great hero! You are a staunch adherent of virtue. I love Shalya and desire to marry him. Don't you think it is your duty to send me back to him?" Hearing that, I immediately arranged for her return to Shalya with all honour. But Shalya refused to accept her as she had been won by someone else. He sent her back again. She said to him, "Bhishma did not want to marry us. It was only for his brother that he took us. He was very noble-minded. As soon as I expressed my wish he sent me back to you in all honour. Will you now discard me?" But Shalya was adamant and sent her back.

Amba was heart-broken. She thought to herself, "Why? Why is fate so cruel to me who has committed no wrong? Should I blame myself or Bhishma? Or my foolish father who arranged the Swayamvara where valour was the only consideration for selection? Shame on my father, shame on Shalya, shame on myself, and shame on Bhishma. Shame on everybody that I was to be given away as the reward of mere valour. No doubt, every person has to face happiness and sorrow in life. But Bhishma has become the chief cause of my sorrow. I should have my revenge on him either through austerities or battle. But few kings venture to fight with that powerful Bhishma." Thinking thus she entered the forest and took shelter in a hermitage. She stayed there for the night and met all the hermits staying in that area. She told them everything in detail — the story of her abduction, her liberation and her abandonment. The hermits, moved by her story, asked her, "O Lady, we are all hermits, spending our time in worship. What help can we offer you?"

She replied, "O sages, I want to achieve by Tapas what could not be achieved by other means." They consulted amongst themselves and tried to dissuade her. "You are a princess. A Tapasvini's life will be unbearably hard for you. Do go back to your father. There is no other proper refuge for you. He will definitely do what is good for you. For either the father or the husband is the refuge of a woman. The husband is a woman's refuge under smooth circumstances and in a difficult situation the father is the refuge." But Amba was adamant. Just then there came the great sage Hotravahana. He listened to her grief silently and said to her, "O my daughter. I am your grandfather. Do not go to your father. I shall show you the way. Go and approach Parasurama, the great sage. He will certainly remove your grief. He will do you justice. If necessary he will even kill Bhishma and avenge the injustice done to you." At that time providence brought Parasurama to that place. He was a great friend of the sage Akritavarna. So he had come there to see him. Amba again related to him her tale of woe. Parasurama heard her patiently. He took pity on her and said, "O fair lady, I will send for Bhishma." But Amba said, "Revered Sir, Bhishma dismissed me as soon as he heard that my mind had already been given in love to someone else. I approached Shalya, but being suspicious of my virtue he rejected me. The root of my distress is Bhishma. Because he took me by force at the Swayamvara this situation has arisen. Now all I desire is revenge, revenge on Bhishma."

Parasurama decided to come to Hastinapura to advise me and make me accept Amba. He took Amba with him and reached Hastinapura. They reached the banks of Saraswati. As soon as Parasurama sent word to me of his arrival, I hurried to the sage and honoured him duly.

Parasurama asked me, "O Bhishma, why did you carry away the girls when you yourself wanted them not. And why did you reject Amba? You have ruined her life. You have touched her. Will any one else now accept her? Quite naturally Shalya has refused her. Accept her honourably now and do justice to her."

I tried my best to convince him but to no avail. He forced me to fight with him since there was no alternative. I reluctantly agreed to fight. At that time my most revered mother, Ganga, appeared and said to me, "What are you doing? I shall go to Parasurama and beg him not to fight." I told her how Parasurama spoke to me. My mother tried her best to stop the fight. But she failed and we had to fight.

It was a long and equal combat. At last my guru had to accept defeat. I went up to him and bowed. He graciously forgave me. He then called Amba and said, "I have done all that I could and I have failed. Take refuge in Bhishma. That is the only course left to you." But Amba would not listen.

She took to a life of severe *tapas* (penance). It went on for a long time.

One day, my mother, Ganga, appeared to her and said, "Why are you engaged in such difficult austerities?" Amba replied "O mother, Bhishma defeated even Parasurama in the battle. To whom else shall I go to plead for me? So I have

taken recourse to perform Tapas, so that I can please Lord Shiva and get a boon from him. The one purpose of my life is to kill Bhishma."

Then, Ganga said, "You are evil minded. With this bad thought in your mind, you will never be able to achieve anything by Tapas. I curse you that you turn into a tortuous river having water only during the rainy season and remaining dry for the other eight months in the year. Your water will be inaccessible and unknown to the people." Cursing Amba thus Ganga disappeared.

When she came to Vatsabhumi, Amba on account of her curse fell down and was changed into a river. By the merit of her austerities, she became a river by only half of her body, while by the other half she remained a maiden as before.

The rishis at Vatsabhumi tried to dissuade her from practising further austerities. But Amba remained adamant and engaged herself further in severe austerities with the one thought of pleasing Lord Shiva.

Finally Lord Shiva appeared before her and said, "Grieve not, my child. In your next birth you will kill Bhishma." But she was not satisfied. She said, "Next birth! What is the use? By then I will not remember my hatred. I may kill him but I will not be able to taste the joy of revenge. I must kill him now." The Lord smiled and said, "Do not worry. In your next birth you will remember your past. You will be born as a daughter of Drupada. Later you will become a man and kill Bhishma."

Amba was impatient to wait. She prepared a pyre and plunged into the fire. Later she was born as Drupada's daughter. When her mother begot a female child she declared it as a male child and kept the fact secret from even her own husband. She was called Shikhandi. Drona educated her. Like the rest of the world he too mistook her to be a man. Years passed. By the kindness of a Yaksha, Amba was able to change her sex and become a man. Thus transformed into a man, he grew up in the house of Drupada with his hatred for me burning like a torch in his heart."

This is the story of Amba, Duryodhana. This is how the son of Drupada is both man and woman. My vow is I cannot fight Shikhandi, really a woman, even if he comes to kill me, facing me directly. This is the vow which I have taken for all time, and it is known to all the world that I will fight with no woman, with no persons who had been woman before, or persons whose names were those of a woman, or those who in appearance seem like a woman. I will not discharge my weapons against any of them. I will not, for this reason, slay Shikhandi."

The time was fast approaching for the war to begin in the early hours of the morning. All retired to sleep.

Thus ends UDYOGA PARVA

Mahabharata for Children

Volume 4

BHISHMA PARVA

&

DRONA PARVA